W9-CEH-117

In Daddy's Arms

I AM TALL

AFRICAN AMERICANS CELEBRATING FATHERS

illustrated by Javaka Steptoe

LEE & LOW BOOKS INC. • New York

Manufactured in China by South China Printing Co.

Book design by Christy Hale
Book production by The Kids at Our House
Art photography by Gamma One Conversions, NYC (Special thanks to Jeith Major)

The editors thank the following for permission to reprint the materials listed below:
E. Ethelbert Miller. "The Things in Black Men's Closets" copyright © 1994 by E. Ethelbert Miller.
Reprinted from *First Light: New and Selected Poems* by E. Ethelbert Miller by permission of
the author and Black Classic Press. • Sonia Sanchez. "My Father's Eyes" copyright © 1985 by
Sonia Sanchez. Reprinted from *I'VE BEEN A WOMAN* by Sonia Sanchez by permission of the
author and Third World Press, Chicago, Illinois. • "Ashanti Proverb" reprinted with permission
from *Kids' Book of Wisdom: Quotes from the African American Tradition,* compiled by Cheryl
and Wade Hudson, copyright © 1996 by Just Us Books, Inc.

The text is set in Antique Olive Roman
The illustrations are rendered in mixed media (see note on page 32)

(HC) 20 19 18 17 16 15 14 13 12
(PB) 15 14 13 12 11 10 9 8 7
First Edition

Library of Congress Cataloging-in-Publication Data
In daddy's arms I am tall: African Americans celebrating fathers/by various African American poets;
illustrated by Javaka Steptoe.—1st ed.
     p.   cm.
Summary: A collection of poems celebrating African American fathers by Angela Johnson,
E. Ethelbert Miller, Carole Boston Weatherford, and others.
ISBN 1-880000-31-8 (hardcover)   ISBN 1-58430-016-7 (paperback)
1. Children's poetry, American—Afro-American authors. 2. Fathers—United States—Juvenile poetry.
3. Afro-American fathers—Juvenile poetry. 4. Men—United States—Juvenile poetry.
5. Afro-American men—Juvenile poetry. [1. Fathers—Poetry. 2. Afro-Americans—Poetry.
3. American poetry—Collections.] I. Steptoe, Javaka.
PS591.N4B46 1997
811.008'03520431—dc21   97-7311   CIP AC
ISBN-13: 978-1-880000-31-1 (hardcover)   ISBN-13: 978-1-58430-016-8 (paperback)

Free Teacher's Guide available at
leeandlow.com/teachers/index.html

Dedicated to my Mother
and the memory of my Father

Special thanks to the energy of
Life, Love, Creativity,
Iman, Pat, everyone who made
this book possible, and of course
the county of Kings,
Brooklyn—J.S.

When you follow in the path of your father,
you learn to walk like him.

—ASHANTI PROVERB

in daddy's arms

in daddy's arms i am tall
& close to the sun & warm
in daddy's arms

in daddy's arms
i can see over the fence out back
i can touch the bottom leaves of the big magnolia tree
in Cousin Sukie's yard
in daddy's arms

in my daddy's arms the moon is close
closer at night time when I can almost touch it
when it grins back at me from the wide twinkling skies

in daddy's arms i am tall
taller than Benny & my friends Ade & George
taller than Uncle Billy
& best of all
i am eye-ball-even-steven with my big brother Jamal

in my daddy's arms
i am strong & dark like him & laughing
happier than the circus clowns
with red painted grins
when daddy spins me round & round
& the whole world is crazy upside down
i am big and strong & proud like him
in daddy's arms
my daddy

—FOLAMI ABIADE

Her Daddy's Hands

His hands, you see, Mama says
were hard and callused.
They worked all day making bricks
that made houses he'd show her
as he flew his noisy old pick-up down the red
Alabama roads.
But on Sundays,
those hands, you see
felt soft,
and would hold my mama's and walk her to church.
Quietly.
Him in black, her in white
along those red Alabama roads.

—ANGELA JOHNSON

Black Father Man

Black Father Man,
the supreme earth dweller.

We are his ripe black crop
at the-beginning-of-the-harvest.
We all bleed his blood
summer-hot and thick
summer-hot and thick
as unstrained milk.
Black Father Man,
the word-music messenger.

We are his grace black note
at the four-beating-of-the-song.
African song,
old song overtaking.
The changing wind;
deft blues breaks free.

Black Father Man,
heal blustering blues,
mend fragmented minds,
teach the maleness,
the maleness, a branching grain,
springing up to shudder the land.
Black Father Man.

—LENARD D. MOORE

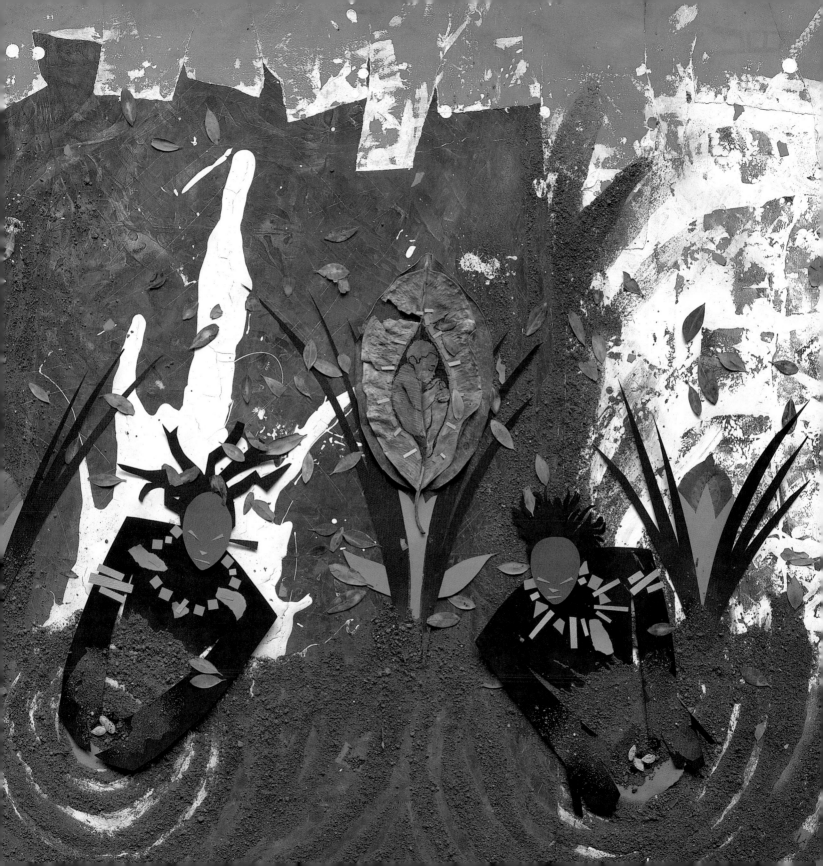

The Farmer

A plot of weeds,
an old grey mule.
Hot sun and sweat
on a bright Southern day.
Strong, stern papa
under a straw hat,
plowing and planting
his whole life away.
His backbone is forged
of African iron
and red Georgia clay.

—CAROLE BOSTON WEATHERFORD

Tickle Tickle

me papa tickle me feet
he call it "finger treat"
me scream and run each time he come
me papa tickle me feet

he tickle me tummy, me chest, me arm
his fingers fly so wild
he say, "Come here, little man.
You my ticklin' chile."

me papa say he love me
me papa look so proud
he say, "Sonny, what a joy
to see you laugh out loud."

he tickle me ribs, me neck, me back
his fingers grow longer each day
me twist and swing and laugh and kick
but he hold me anyway

me eyes, they water
me throat be sore
me weak, me dizzy
but me want more

he throw me high up in the air
and catch me from behind
me say, "Go higher!" and he say,
"Don't you know you're mine?"

me papa tickle me feet
he call it "finger treat"
me scream and run (but OH, WHAT FUN!)
when papa tickle me feet

—DAKARI HRU

Lightning Jumpshot

Daddy's voice thunders
he shoots a lightning jumpshot
through a sweaty storm

—MICHAEL BURGESS

The Things in Black Men's Closets

on the top shelf
of the closet
is the hat my father
wears on special occasions
it rests next to the large jar
he saves his pennies in

his head is always bare
when i see him walking
in the street

i once sat in his bedroom
watching him search
between sweaters and suits
looking for something missing
a tie perhaps

then he stopped
and slowly walked to the closet
took the hat from the shelf

i sat on the bed
studying his back
waiting for him to turn
and tell me who died

—E. ETHELBERT MILLER

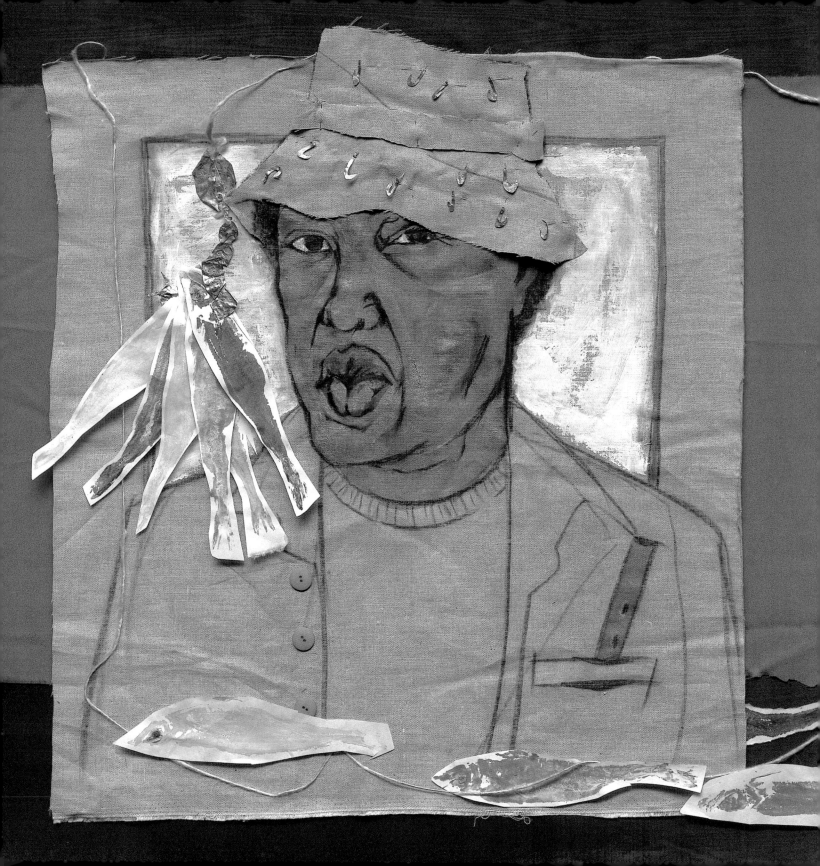

My Granddaddy Is My Daddy Too

Nobody has a granddaddy
Like my granddaddy.
Nobody's granddaddy
Is named Douglas Jasper Blue.
Nobody's grandfather
Has smoked a pipe for fifty years
And always has tobacco to chew.
Nobody else's big daddy
Can carve whistles out of wood.
Nobody's else's grandfather
Has feet almost two feet long.
Only my grandpa
Can catch fifteen fish in a day.
And he makes up his very own silly songs.

Nobody has a granddaddy
Like my granddaddy.
I'm so lucky
That he's my one and only Daddy.

—DINAH JOHNSON

Promises

Dear Daddy,
I'm sorry I did not do what you told me to do.
If I do better
Can I still be your little boy?

Dear Son,
You will be
My little boy
For all of your little-boy days.
And when
You are no longer a little boy
I will still be your daddy.

—DAVID A. ANDERSON

Seeds

You drew pictures of life
with your words.
I listened and ate these words you said
to grow up strong.
Like the trees, I grew,
branches, leaves, flowers, and then the fruit.

I became the words I ate in you.
For better or worse
the apple doesn't fall far from the tree.

—JAVAKA STEPTOE

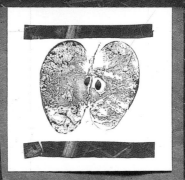

Artist to Artist

I write books, now, because my father wanted
to be an artist when he grew up & he was good
at it, too. Drew people with meat on their bones
in flesh-colored tones from my 64-colors box
of crayons. But
every night—& sometimes even weekends & holidays—
he dressed in the blue uniform & black shoes
of many other fathers who also weren't doctors or lawyers,
teachers or preachers, & rode the 10:00 p.m. bus
to the downtown post office. Sorted mail by zip code—
60620, 60621, 60622. He sorted mail all night &
into the day because we had bills to pay. For 30 years
my father rode the bus feeling black and blue. He
never drew & his degrees in art & education sat
hardening on a shelf along with his oils
& acrylics. But
along with his gapped teeth, his bow legs & his first name
with an A at the end, he gave me the urge to create
characters with meat on their bones, in flesh-colored tones
written in words as vivid as a 64-colors box of crayons.
I write, he drew. Daddy, thank you!
& now that you're
retired . . .

        . . .what do you want to be?

—DAVIDA ADEDJOUMA

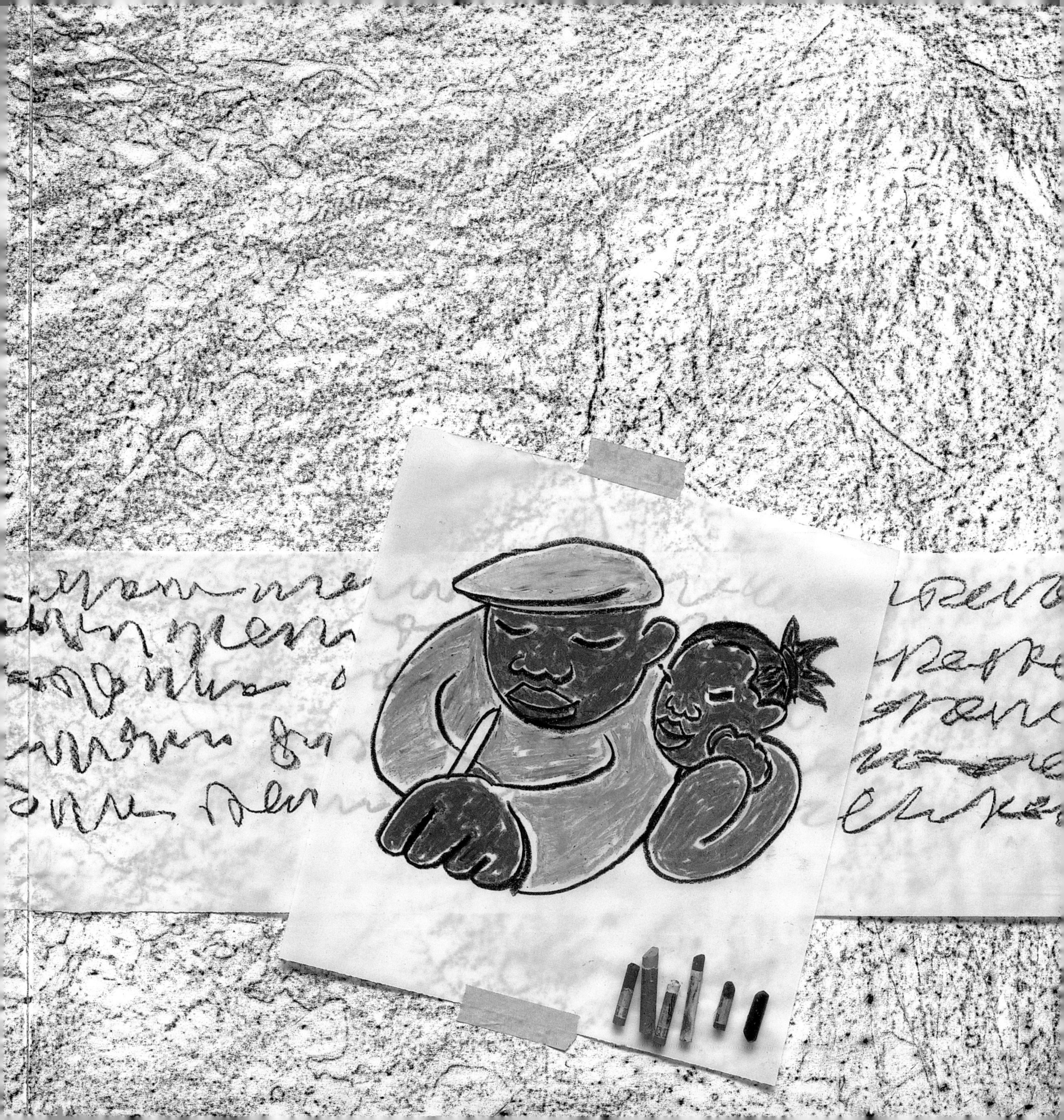

My Father's Eyes

I have looked into
    my father's eyes and seen an
    african sunset.

—SONIA SANCHEZ

ABOUT THE POETS

Folami Abiade's poetry has appeared in several anthologies and a collection, *There's Magic in the Dust: we don't need no aspirin*. Ms. Abiade is a member of Atlanta's First World Writers, and lives in Decatur, Georgia.

Davida Adedjouma is a writer, actor, and teacher. She is the author of *Last Summer*, a collection of short stories, and the editor of *The Palm of My Heart: Poetry by African American Children*, winner of the 1997 Coretta Scott King Illustrator Honor Award and the 1996 Reading Magic Award from *Parenting* magazine. Ms. Adedjouma lives in New York City.

David A. Anderson is a writer, storyteller, and lecturer for African and Afro-American Studies at the State University of New York in Brockport. His picture book for children, *The Origin of Life on Earth: An African Creation Myth*, won the 1993 Coretta Scott King Illustrator Honor Award. He and his wife live in Rochester, New York, and are the parents of three grown children.

Michael Burgess is a writer and actor who was born and raised in Myrtle Beach, South Carolina, where he lives with his wife and two daughters. "Lightning Jumpshot" is Mr. Burgess' first published poem for children.

Dakari Hru (1952 - 1994) was a poet, writer, and storyteller. His picture books for children included *Joshua's Masai Mask* and *The Magic Moonberry Jump Ropes*, and his poetry was featured in the anthology *Make a Joyful Sound*.

Angela Johnson is the author of over 15 books for young readers, including the picture books *Do Like Kyla* and *The Rolling Store*, and the novels *Toning the Sweep* and *Humming Whispers*. Her national awards include the Coretta Scott King Award, the Ezra Jack Keats Award, and the PEN American/Norma Klein Award.

Dinah Johnson is an associate professor of English at the University of South Carolina. Her books include *The Best of the Brownies Book* and *Telling Tales: The Pedagogy and Promise of African American Literature for Youth*. Ms. Johnson lives in Columbia, South Carolina, with her family.

E. Ethelbert Miller is the author of *Where are the Love Poems for Dictators?* and *First Light: Selected and New Poems*, and the editor of *In Search of Color Everywhere: A Collection of African American Poetry*, which won the 1994 PEN Oakland Josephine Miles Award. Mr. Miller is the director of the African American Resource Center at Howard University. He lives in Washington, D.C. with his wife and their two children.

Lenard D. Moore's collections of poetry include *Forever Home* and *The Open Eye*. A native of North Carolina, Mr. Moore works as a graduate teaching assistant and conducts poetry workshops throughout the state, in addition to his writing. Mr. Moore lives in Raleigh, North Carolina, with his wife and their daughter.

Sonia Sanchez is the author of 13 books, including *I've Been a Woman, Homegirls and Handgrenades,* and *Does Your House Have Lions?* Among her many awards and honors are a National Endowment for the Arts grant and the Peace and Freedom Award from the Women's International League for Peace and Freedom. Ms. Sanchez is Laura Carnell Professor of English and Women's Studies at Temple University.

Carole Boston Weatherford is the author of several books for children, including the picture book *Juneteenth Jamboree*. Her awards for poetry include the 1995 North Carolina Writers' Network Harperprint Chapbook Competition. She lives in High Point, North Carolina, with her husband and their two children.

ABOUT THE ILLUSTRATIONS

The images in this book were created with a variety of materials and techniques. In addition to torn paper, cut paper with pastel, and appliqué, the collages and paintings contain many found objects, such as scraps from a tin ceiling ("The Farmer"); floorboards salvaged from a building renovation in Brooklyn, New York ("Lightning Jumpshot"); real fish dipped in paint ("My Grandaddy Is My Daddy Too"); and coins, insects, seashells, soil, barrettes, buttons, burlap, clothing, and fabric scraps. The child's drawing in the cover art was contributed by the artist's youngest sister.

The size of the original art ranges from small to very large. The smallest piece (pictured on the dedication page) fits easily in the palm of an adult's hand. The largest piece ("My Father's Eyes") is approximately ten feet long and five feet high.